YOUR KNOWLEDGE HAS VALUE

- We will publish your bachelor's and
  master's thesis, essays and papers

- Your own eBook and book -
  sold worldwide in all relevant shops

- Earn money with each sale

Upload your text at www.GRIN.com
and publish for free

Akin Awoyode

About the need of building green

GRIN Publishing

Bibliographic information published by the German National Library:

The German National Library lists this publication in the National Bibliography; detailed bibliographic data are available on the Internet at http://dnb.dnb.de .

This book is copyright material and must not be copied, reproduced, transferred, distributed, leased, licensed or publicly performed or used in any way except as specifically permitted in writing by the publishers, as allowed under the terms and conditions under which it was purchased or as strictly permitted by applicable copyright law. Any unauthorized distribution or use of this text may be a direct infringement of the author s and publisher s rights and those responsible may be liable in law accordingly.

Imprint:

Copyright © 2015 GRIN Verlag GmbH
Print and binding: Books on Demand GmbH, Norderstedt Germany
ISBN: 978-3-656-89552-7

This book at GRIN:

http://www.grin.com/en/e-book/289216/about-the-need-of-building-green

GRIN - Your knowledge has value

Since its foundation in 1998, GRIN has specialized in publishing academic texts by students, college teachers and other academics as e-book and printed book. The website www.grin.com is an ideal platform for presenting term papers, final papers, scientific essays, dissertations and specialist books.

Visit us on the internet:

http://www.grin.com/

http://www.facebook.com/grincom

http://www.twitter.com/grin_com

Table of contents

INTRODUCTION

Our way of life is killing us. Our buildings consume over 40% of our energy and resources and their use represents 70% of our total consumption (Rabin 2005). It's further stressed that the environmental damage caused in the last hundred years is a direct result from how our buildings are built. Architects, designers, and all building professionals are in a position to affect great change on our environment, more so, than any other group, since our buildings are responsible for most of the damage. "Green building"(also known as "sustainable," "ecological," and "eco-designed") is a way of looking at buildings in terms of reducing energy use, conserving water, improving indoor air quality, and reducing dependence on our natural resources. Although the basic concepts for green building have been around for decades, it has only been in the last few years that we have seen this explosive growth in the greening of the construction industry" (Rabin 2005).Since buildings account for one-sixth of the world's fresh water withdrawals, one-quarter of its wood harvest, and two-fifths of its material and energy flows, (Roodman,& Lenssen,1995).Therefore it's the duty of a reasonable property industry to balance environmental, social and economic issues to ensure a viable and valuable industry for future generations.

DEFINITION OF A SUISTAINABLE PROPERTY.

There are many definitions of sustainable property that exist, but none is entirely satisfactory. Sustainable buildings may be equated to 'green buildings'. For example Kats (2003) regards to them as synonymous and as buildings that "use key resources like energy, water, materials and land more efficiently than buildings that are just built to code." This according to Sayce and Ellison (2004) implies an environmental interpretation of sustainability; implicit within Kats' definition is that sustainability is a moving goal with 'green' or sustainable being reserved for those that are built 'beyond compliance natural light and indoor air quality. Additionally United Nations World Commission on Environment and Development 1987 gives the definition of a sustainable development as development that meets the needs of the present without compromising the ability of future generations to meet their own needs.

Green buildings, (according to Governor's Green Government Council) are designed, constructed and operated to achieve sustainability, water efficiency, energy, resources and indoor environment quality goals A green building is one whose construction and lifetime of operation assure the healthiest possible environment while representing the most efficient and least disruptive use of land, water, energy and resources.

NEED FOR A SUSTAINABLE BUILDING.

Sustainability has not only been described by many research as an investment for the future but sustainable property can as well contribute to the wellbeing of inhabitants, according to Wittneben (2014), Real Estate is responsible for the majority of Europe's carbon emissions. He further stated that the real estate industry will be at the forefront of any reduction in carbon and other sustainability improvements. Wittneben (2014)."With most of us spending more than 90% of our time indoors, green building is the healthy, common sense choice for a better life. In traditional construction, the quality of our indoor environment is often far more polluted than outdoor one due to the building materials, inadequate lighting, and a variety of other variables". (Rabin 2005).

Another need for sustainability in real estate is the change in the lease pattern, in a survey carried out in UK Sayce and Ellison (2004) reported that the change in the lease pattern or rather the relationship change in landlord and tenants over time calls for sustainability in property sector. In the report Sayce and Ellison (2004), Lawrence (2005) stated that the standard commercial lease has long been constructed to reduce risk for the landlord. Two particular provision according to them, combined with lease length have been important; First the landlord usually placed liability on tenants on Repairs (including structural repairs and any upgrade required by law); this on the side of the landlord will protect him or her on any deficiency in the building during the lease. Secondly according to their survey report, the regular upward on rent review as a clause which ensures that owners are protected against the fall in the value of the building during lease and can only be discovered at the end of the lease that the property value have depreciated because of its failure to meet the requirement of the new tenant under legislation.

DRIVERS OF SUSTAINABLE PROPERTY

Legislation: The treat of legislation according to Sarah, S., Louise, E., & Philip, P., (2005), in a survey conducted across UK has been described as the first driver of sustainability in property sector, in the report summary, treat by legislators in various countries (UK for instance) has been observed to be the key driver in changing attitude of investors to possibly understand the financial worth implication of sustainability agenda. Furthermore, the last decade has seen substantial shift in attitudes towards sustainability, not only has sustainable development gained more attention within political debate between national and international level but has also become an important part of co-operate agenda in development economics. (Sarah, S., Louise, E., & Philip, P., (2005)).

3

ENERGY EFFICIENCY: Energy efficiency is another driver of sustainability in property sector, because the ability for a building to perform or rather its efficiency is limited to how the building is designed, engineered constructed, operated and maintained. (IFMA 2010) In order to achieve greater energy efficiency in a building depends on so many factors which include the building envelop, system types, energy end use, e. plugs loads and the operation of the building with regards to maintenance practices. (IFMA 2010).

In their survey in 2010, IFMA foundation established that simple strategies to reduce heating and cooling loads include appropriate insulation, optimizing window glazing area, minimizing the filtration of air outside and the use of opaque roofing materials. Depending on how much daylight penetrates through the window into the interior space, the report mentioned that using common design features will give room the enhancement of natural daylight into the building through the use of skylight, light shelves tubular day lighting and other means of day light harvesting which will not only sustain a building but will also reduce the cost of energy consumption. (IMFA 2010)

Similarly, in comparison IMFA report in 2010 on energy efficiency of a building has assumed that the energy cost of a building can be driven by so many factors among which are: Geographical, Climate and building type location. Even though energy cost has been argued by many professionals to the most controlled able expenses of any property unlike other expenses like taxes and insurance but if sustainability in this sector find its way globally we would not only pay less on energy consumption we might have a lot energy saved for the generations to come. For instance CEBECS (2003) in their energy saving survey arrived at the consumption of energy is about \$1.09 per sq. ft. for all US building, \$11.73 per sq/m for office building, various survey in US on energy saving assumed prices of energy has increased over the last 7years. Ciocheti & McGowan (2009) rated the average commercial energy cost to have increased by 25% since 2000.Hence it's clear that the energy efficiency in a building is a pressing issue globally which according to IMFA (2010) report confirmed that building and industry energy consumption is growing even more intense and there is a call for sustainability in this regards

OCCUPIER: The agitation of occupiers on sustainable homes cannot be overlooked when talking about drivers of sustainability in real estate. Occupiers according to Wittneben (2014) in a survey where over 100 stakeholder in real estate investment participated Emphasized that as liquidity improve on both the investors and occupier market a trend toward sustainability is seeing,. For occupiers as long as energy costs are very small fraction of rental value, they are

4

not likely to be a crucial decision in their selection. See,Y., & TU (2011) in their survey report on Singapore property market have seen occupiers willingness to pay more on sustainable building once delivered and lived in, since they can verify the "green" claims by checking the electricity bills which implies that most of the occupiers in Asia, (or in Singapore precisely) are willing to pay for sustainable building after physical delivery and testing of the unit, so on the part of the investor it might likely to have a green lease with conditions if possible. The stand of occupiers would be discussed further in the circle of blame.

BREAKING THE CIRCLE OF BLAME

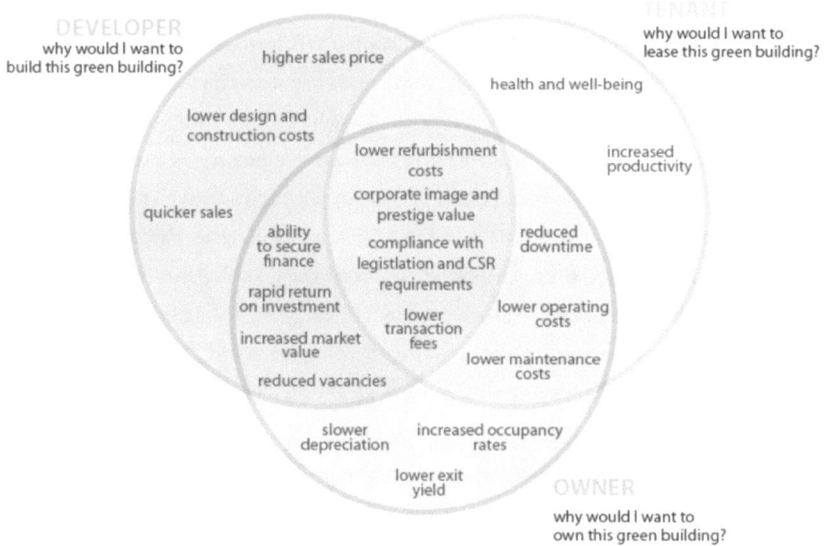

Source: (World Green Building Council, 2013)

Occupier. 'We would like to have more sustainable buildings but there is too little choice'. This statement is the general opinion of occupier of real estate globally which has resulted in so many survey carried out across the world just to verify and affirm the position of occupier on sustainable buildings. Taking the report of Lasselle (2008) in a survey where over 400 occupiers participated globally it's clearly known that occupiers want sustainable buildings they are even willing to pay more for sustainable property but the availability is viewed by occupiers as sporadic. According to Lassele (2008) survey where over 47% of occupiers responded globally it was seen that the need for sustainable building by occupiers is not the question anymore, it's even the question of when will it be a critical issue, the answer to the 47% respondent is that sustainability is already a critical issue to them right now. To over quarter of remaining respondent arguing that sustainability will be an issue to them in short time, basically in 2 years' time. As regards to whether or not sustainable buildings would cost more and what it's like to be the additional cost, according to their report Lassele (2008) said that occupiers are pragmatic in respect of the additional cost incurred by owners and developer in designing, delivering and certifying a building to BREEAM or LEED standards. Their survey report further expressed that over 70% of North American respondent assumed that sustainable building will cost up to 10% more than the traditional building, a few percentage according to their report suggested that the cost for delivering a green building might be in excess of 10%, 11% of the total respondents maintained that sustainable building might actually cost less or more than conventional product. But whatever the case of how much it cost, occupiers showed a huge interest in sustainable property acquisition globally, evidence of which is shown in the report of this survey where two-third of respondent from North America, Asia Pacific, Australasia and EMEA are willing to pay a premium for sustainable buildings. 74% of occupiers who responded from North America are willing to pay a premium of 1-10%, a small percentage from this region are willing to pay a bit more in excess of 10%.Due to the market scarcity of sustainable property in Pacific Asia, 16 % of respondent from this region are even willing to pay double digit premium.(Lassele 2008)

Below tables shows occupiers interest as to the demand time for sustainable building

(Source: Laselle 2008.Global trends in sustainable real estate: occupier's perspective)

	EMEA	NORT-AMERICA	ASIA-PACIFIC	AUSTRALASIA
Critical now	62%	44%	42%	52%
Critical within 1-2 years	23%	35%	20%	23%

Below shows occupiers willingness to pay for sustainable building.

(Source: Laselle 2008. Global trends in sustainable real estate: occupier's perspective)

Premium	EMEA	NORTH AMERICA	ASIA-PACIFIC	AUSTRALASIA
Same or less	34	23	36	32
1-10%	64	74	48	61
>10%	2	3	16	7

INVESTORS: Its evident that sustainability in real estate is an increasingly important issue for investors, even in a falling investment market; this is contrary to a commonly proffered view that sustainability will diminish in importance as economic circumstance worsen.*(GVA Grimley).*In this report it was mentioned that investors of property have clear views about the importance of sustainability in their decision - making when selling and purchasing assets, it's clearly started that occupiers demand and government legislation(future) is like to drive investors hard into deciding about sustainable property investment. According to a report ''Green to Gold' 'A survey conducted by *GVA Grimley*, it was discovered that smart investors appreciate that careful consideration of sustainable property should mean focusing on enhancing values; which could be achieved by carefully attending to physical attributes of a building, as well as other future-proofing issues such as those which are brought about by change in legislation. In this survey *GVA Grimley* asked various investors how important they thought sustainability is to their decision making in property segment, answers varies from 'no importance,'' some importance'', equal importance'', or over-riding importance''. The result of *GVA Grimley* survey saw investors of 18% responding that sustainability is of no importance to them when considering which properties are to be sold, 58% responded that they are of some importance, while 24% maintained that they are of equal importance with other factors, positively according to the report of this survey no respondent stated that sustainability is of over-riding importance.

''Sustainability; Investment risk or opportunity?''. This is the question most investors were asked during a survey on New Zealand property market, Myers, Reed &Robinson(2008) confirmed that even though investors in this survey believed that if they take the risk of sustainability and become owners of sustainable buildings before the market has settled, they are positioning themselves as a leaders and this will lead to a significant returns in the future because tenants/occupiers global demand for sustainable buildings is growing in both private and public sector which among others, the reasons for them to pursue sustainability. In Georgia,M.,Richard,,R.& Jon, R.(2008) survey report it was stated that 64% of investors are ready to pay but to investors there is the lack of research and documentations on what will it cost them to own a sustainable property and this remains a crucial question. Investors in New Zealand believes that sustainable buildings would probably yield in high rent, reduced vacancy, premium or government tenants, reduced operating cost all of which they believed according to Georgia,M.,Richard.& Jon, R.(2008) report would yield a huge return of investment and the value of property. Therefore the perception that the investors are ready to pay premium is based on the financial return they would receive. On the other hand 36% of the respondent's investors in this survey argued not to pay more for a sustainable property as according to them the market is not yet mature enough to determine how much they should be paid by occupier as a return on such investment. (Georgia,M.,Richard,R.& Jon,R. 2008)

DEVELOPERS: The development of sustainable building has been gradually noticed as important for achieving the goal of a green society. ,Li and Quigley (2012) said that the construction and operation of a building accounts for about 40% of the worldwide energy consumptions. In their survey taking Singapore for example, it was learnt that a positive premium does not guarantee a positive economic return to developers. The conflicting or mismatch from occupier on demand for sustainable building as regard the energy savings according to developers in Singapore can only be financially sustainable if the "green price premium' is too large enough compare to additional 'green cost' to provide meaningful economic return to investors and developers. However, Li and Quigley (2012) considered the fact that most developers in Asia always built dwelling units which are immediately sold to household or pre sold before being completed which makes the lump-sum payment from household buyers be used by developers as rewards on any green building investment which is probably possible to cause a mismatch in the timing of the cost and benefits.

According to Green mark system (2005) (Purposely established organization to evaluate sustainability in relation to the energy efficiency of a building), globally there have been series of research to outline the opinion of developers as regards to sustainable property, when asked developers in U.S (Michigan) in a survey report by Deng and Wu (2013) ''Developers said they can build greenhouse if the demand were greater' 'But reality according to the report is that demand for green building in Michigan is rapidly growing and building company are accumulating data on the benefit of green practices. Developers in Michigan according to this survey said green buildings are too large commitment for them but the reality shows that sustainability of real estate is a feasible design. It shows that green development practice can range from simple to intricate.(Deng and Wu 2013)

RISK OF SUSTAINABLE BUILDING

There are some legal risk on sustainable building as regards to the investor/owner and the occupier/tenants relationship according to Masters and Musitano JR (2007).They include:

1. Fraud
2. Negligence
3. Breach of Contract.

In general terms there are other risks which are outside legal performance which include:

Potential Risk

Contract Recommendation

Tort Recommendation

Government Recommendation

Regulatory Risk

Diving Energy retrofit.

Mitigating sustainable property risk.

- According to Masters and Musitano JR (2007) builders can manage user's expectations and decrease their liability and exposures by employing a wide range of operation and legal risk mitigation techniques.
- Use of clear definition and performance standard contracts.
- Builders must implement a plan that is comprehensive and integrated
- All terms must be clearly define in the context of transaction.

CONCLUSION.

In submission, it's clearly seen by data evidence and opinion that all stakeholders in real estate have individual desire, concern and role to ensure sustainability in property sector, it's not just a say that there might like be a future legislation change which will support sustainability giving the real estate chance of green development. In order to break the circle of blame it's important for property market analyst to be accurate in figures, findings and all other data evidence to orientate the developer who according to research are to take the lead in building green for investors to purchase since occupiers are willing to acquire and ready to pay premium (where possible).

References

CEBECS. (2003) "Energy efficiency of a green building;(online) Available at http://books.google.co.uk/books?id=eA91AgAAQBAJ&pg=PA59&lpg=PA59&dq=CBECS+ (2003)+ENERGY+EFFICIENCY+OF+A+GREEN+BUILDING&source=bl&ots=MMdcAX Aa0j&sig=oC9bS_9RwDqvZlaFTAwUEt48Sv0&hl=en&sa=X&ei=mWxOVJn_IaiV7Aah_oH ABQ&ved=0CDQQ6AEwAg#v=onepage&q=CBECS%20(2003)%20ENERGY%20EFFICIE NCY%20OF%20A%20GREEN%20BUILDING&f=false (Accessed 16& 27th October 2014)

CIOCHETI&McGowan (2009) "Value beyond cost; How to underwrite sustainable properties (online) Available at http://books.google.co.uk/books?id=EU6lWOsatSwC&pg=PA81&lpg=PA81&dq=CIOCHE TTI+McGowan+(2009)+on+sustainability&source=bl&ots=4QDnbgUfZ7&sig=0LQJ_1qh mykUv_-94A1BiHHqWJ4&hl=en&sa=X&ei=Jm5OVNjyCcOp7Abyv4CgCg&ved=0CCEQ6AEwAA# v=onepage&q=CIOCHETTI%20McGowan%20(2009)%20on%20sustainability&f=false (Accessed 16 & 27th Octomber 2014)

Dominique, H. Andrew, W M. and Margaret, B ."The Australian Journal of Construction Economics and Building [Vol5, No2J]' (ONLINE) Available at http://epress.lib.uts.edu.au/journals/index.php/AJCEB/article/viewFile/2956/3128 (Accessed on 14th&27th October 2014)

Emily, R. (2005) "Top Ten Green Building Questions" (Online) Available at http://www.greenbiz.com/blog/2005/09/15/ask-green-architect-top-ten-green-building-questions (Accessed 15th & 27 October 2014)

GVA Grimley () "Our approach to sustainability" (online) Available at http://www.google.co.uk/url?sa=t&rct=j&q=&esrc=s&frm=1&source=web&cd=1&ved=0 CCEQFjAA&url=http%3A%2F%2Fwww.gva.co.uk%2Fenvironmental-services%2Four-approach-to-sustainability%2F&ei=b3ROVMyFMZGP7AbZk4HwBw&usg=AFQjCNFNbvE47tmSYTKXr ELNF_BPBkCNzQ&bvm=bv.77880786,d.ZWU (Accessed 19th&27th October 2014)

IFMA. (2010)."The Economics of Sustainability in commercial real estate'; (online) Available at http://www.cleanlink.com/pdf/casestudieswhitepapers/IFMA_0810.pdf (Accessed 27th October 2014)

Jones, L.(2008)"Global Trends in Sustainable Real Estate: An Occupier's Perspective" (Online) Available at http://www.joneslanglasalle.com/csr/SiteCollectionDocuments/Global_Sustainability_Feb08. pdf (Accessed 15th&27th October 2014)

Jeffrey D. M and John R. M, Jr (2007) "Managing Liability Risks in Green Construction" (Online) Available at *http://www.americanbar.org/content/dam/aba/publications/rpte_ereport/2008/february/rober ts_green.authcheckdam.pdf (Accessed 14th,15th,27th October 2014)*

Georgia, M .Richard.& Jon, R.(2008) "Investor Perception of the Business Case for Sustainable Office Buildings: evidence from New Zealand" (online) Available at http://www.prres.net/Proceedings/..%5CPapers%5CMyers_Investor_Perception_Of_The_Bu siness_Case.pdf (Accessed 15th&27th October 2014)

Sayce and Ellison (2004) "The Sustainable Property Appraisal Project'' (online) Available at http://kueprints3.kingston.ac.uk/1435/1/Sustainable_Property_Appraisal_Project.pdf (Accessed on 16th&27th October 2014)

Stephanie, D W. (2014) "TOWARDS A GREENER FUTURE;DLA Piper's market report on sustainable real estate"(Online) Available at http://www.dlapiper.com/~/media/Files/Insights/Publications/2014/03/towardsagreenerfutur e.pdf (Accessed on 16 & 27th October 2014)

Yongheng ,D. and Jing W. (2013) "Economic Returns to Residential Green Building Investment: The Developers' Perspective" (ONLINE) Available at http://www.ires.nus.edu.sg/workingpapers/IRES2013-016.pdf (Accessed on 16th & 27th October 2014)